Predator
and Prey

THIS EDITION
Editorial Management by Oriel Square
Produced for DK by WonderLab Group LLC
Jennifer Emmett, Erica Green, Kate Hale, *Founders*

Editors Grace Hill Smith, Libby Romero, Maya Myers, Michaela Weglinski;
Photography Editors Kelley Miller, Annette Kiesow, Nicole DiMella; **Managing Editor** Rachel Houghton;
Designers Project Design Company; **Researcher** Michelle Harris; **Copy Editor** Lori Merritt;
Indexer Connie Binder; **Proofreader** Larry Shea; **Reading Specialist** Dr. Jennifer Albro;
Curriculum Specialist Elaine Larson

Published in the United States by DK Publishing
1745 Broadway, 20th Floor, New York, NY 10019

Copyright © 2023 Dorling Kindersley Limited
DK, a Division of Penguin Random House LLC
23 24 25 26 10 9 8 7 6 5 4 3 2 1
001–334086–July/2023

All rights reserved.

Without limiting the rights under the copyright reserved above, no part of this publication may be reproduced, stored in or introduced into a retrieval system, or transmitted, in any form, or by any means (electronic, mechanical, photocopying, recording, or otherwise), without the prior written permission of the copyright owner.
Published in Great Britain by Dorling Kindersley Limited

A catalog record for this book
is available from the Library of Congress.
HC ISBN: 978-0-7440-7440-6
PB ISBN: 978-0-7440-7441-3

DK books are available at special discounts when purchased in bulk for sales promotions, premiums, fundraising, or educational use. For details, contact: DK Publishing Special Markets, 1745 Broadway, 20th Floor, New York, NY 10019
SpecialSales@dk.com

Printed and bound in China

The publisher would like to thank the following for their kind permission to reproduce their images:
a=above; c=center; b=below; l=left; r=right; t=top; b/g=background

123RF.com: Chainarong 7tr, Eric Isselee / isselee 33tr, Brian Kinney 25cra, lantapix 33crb, Nico Smit / EcoSnap 31tl; **Alamy Stock Photo:** Andrew Newman Nature Pictures 19t, Avalon.red / Stephen Dalton 19cr, 40cra, David Fleetham 21tr, Gallo Images / Heinrich van den Berg 31tr, Jeffrey Isaac Greenberg 13+ 30tl, imageBROKER / Mathieu Foulquie 21b, Stephen Dalton / Minden Pictures 13tl, Louise Murray 20t, WorldFoto 34b; **Dorling Kindersley:** Liberty's Owl, Raptor and Reptile Centre, Hampshire, UK 15tr; **Dreamstime.com:** Andreykuzmin 22-23, Muhammad Annurmal 14tl, Andrew Astbury 43tr, Rinus Baak 38tl, Beataaldridge 18-19b, Belizar 16cl, Cathywithers 32tl, Razvan Cornel Constantin 41cr, Neal Cooper 17cra, Davemhuntphotography 23tr, Lgor Dolgov / Id1974 29tr, Judit Dombovari 14tr, Dennis Donohue 39bc, Dssimages 14br, Daniel Dunca 11cra, Ecophoto 17crb, Eivaisla 39crb, Lane Erickson 12tl, Farinoza 15tl, Frank Fichtmueller 18cla, Jakob Fischer 35tr, Simon Fletcher 22br, Jan Martin Will / Freezingpictures 37crb, Yun Gao 45crb, David Havel 15cr, Eric Isselee 1b, Isselee 8clb, Izanbar 30cl, Cathy Keifer 40bc, 41t, Sergey Korotkov 34tl, Geoffrey Kuchera 12br, Matthijs Kuijpers 14clb, Lucaar 31cra, Bruce Macqueen 22r, Amelia Martin 42tl, Vaclav Matous 6tr, James Mattil 42r, Wayne Mckown 41crb, Arno Meintjes 16br, Meisterphotos 30br, Meoita 6tl, Michal Ninger 44-45b, Matee Nuserm 40cl, Marc Parsons 40crb, Martin Pelanek 26cl, Petrp 25tr, Stu Porter 9tr, 10-11, 32-33b, Pzaxe 7crb, Pongphan Ruengchai 28cla, Yerbolat Shadrakhov 26-27t, Slowmotiongli 42clb, Springdt313 34cl, Staphy 36-37t, Johannes Gerhardus Swanepoel 11tr, Tarpan 35cb, Tirrasa 7cr, Mogens Trolle 10tl, Anuraj R V 29tr, Vaeenma 11br, Vladvitek 38clb, Wirestock 8-9b, Nora Yusuf 36tl, Rudmer Zwerver 38-39cb; **Fotolia:** dundanim 25br, Eric Isselee 43crb; **Getty Images:** imageBROKER / Robert Haasmann 12-13b, Raimund Linke 43tl, Moment / By Eve Livesey 24cla, Moment / Photo. Keith Draycott 13crb, RooM / ronikurniawan 13tr, The Image Bank / Jay Dickman 4-5; **Getty Images / iStock:** ANDREYGUDKOV 3cb, Gerald Corsi 28tl, E+ / Andrew Peacock 35tl, E+ / John Morrison 6b, Geoffrey Reynaud 44clb, Ted Smith 37tr, WhitcombeRD 23bl; **naturepl.com:** Emanuele Biggi 25l; **Science Photo Library:** Andrew J. Martinez 29b, Merlintuttle.org 40tl, Spencer Sutton 39tl; **Shutterstock.com:** Craig Cordier 17tl, Federico.Crovetto 24br, Josh McPhail 31crb, Sklo Studio 20clb, Alen thien 22cla

Cover images: *Front*: **Dreamstime.com:** Yasushitanikado

All other images © Dorling Kindersley
For more information see: www.dkimages.com

For the curious
www.dk.com

Level 4

Predator
and Prey

Ruth A. Musgrave

CONTENTS

- **6**   Predator Versus Prey
- **12**   Keep Away
- **18**   Out of Sight
- **24**   It's a Trap!
- **30**   No Contest
- **34**   Polar Predators

38	Dinner in the Dark
42	Finding Balance
46	Glossary
47	Index
48	Quiz

Honey Badgers
Honey badgers' thick skin helps protect them from their venomous prey, like bees and cobras.

Brown Bears
Brown bears eat fish, moose, and caribou. They also eat roots, grass, and bulbs.

PREDATOR VERSUS PREY

Predators—animals that eat other animals, or prey—sometimes succeed in their hunt for food. Other times, the prey survives.

These battles happen in every environment on Earth.

Predators can be large like brown bears or whale sharks. Or they can be small, like ladybugs or weasels.

While an arctic fox hunts for rodents scurrying beneath the snow, flying eagles hunt the fox from above.

Predators have an important job. Without predators, prey would not have anything to limit their populations. If prey populations were to become too big, the prey would eat and eat. Eventually, they would run out of food or places to live. Without predators, there would be an imbalance in the ecosystem.

Predators work hard to get their food, but they are not successful every time they hunt. Prey are not always easy to catch. For every skill or strength a predator has, its prey has a comparable one to avoid becoming lunch.

In a balanced ecosystem, there are more prey animals than predators. If predators are too good at their job, they run out of food. And if prey are too good at their job, predators starve.

A healthy habitat requires a balance between predators and prey.

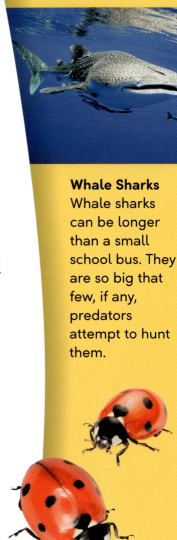

Whale Sharks
Whale sharks can be longer than a small school bus. They are so big that few, if any, predators attempt to hunt them.

Ladybugs
A ladybug can eat as many as 5,000 tiny insects in about a year.

Heads Up
Stallions, or male zebras, alert the herd to danger and fight predators to give the females and young time to escape.

On the Hunt
Hyenas, cheetahs, and wild dogs hunt zebras.

Hiding in Stripes
Zebras' stripes might help confuse predators.

Predators and prey use all their skills to triumph.

The lion approaches the zebras. Slowly. The big cat hides behind the grass and crouches close to the ground.

A zebra stallion raises its head. The other zebras stop grazing. All are alert for danger. The lion freezes. It doesn't take its eyes off the prey. Minutes tick by. The zebras have relaxed. One has wandered slightly away from the rest.

The distance between the lion and zebra is critical. The zebra has a chance of escaping if the lion attacks too soon. The lion takes off. So does the startled zebra. The cat sprints to get in front of it to cut off its escape.

Lions have size and strength. So do zebras. Zebras are fast. So are lions. A lion's legs can grab and take down a zebra. A zebra's kick can kill a lion. Both are tough. Both want to survive.

The lion must be stronger, faster, and quicker than the animal it hunts.

Herd Protection
Zebras live in small groups. Sometimes, these groups join with others to create a herd of several hundred zebras.

Lions hunt in the morning or evening and rest during the hottest part of the day.

Missed Meals
Lions catch their prey less than 30 percent of the time.

Size on Their Side
A zebra can weigh twice as much as a male or female lion.

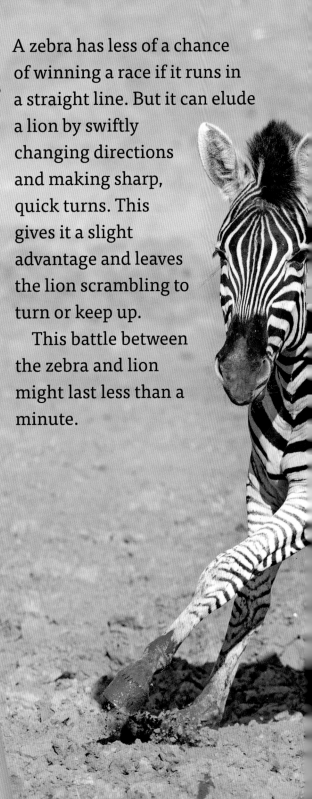

A zebra has less of a chance of winning a race if it runs in a straight line. But it can elude a lion by swiftly changing directions and making sharp, quick turns. This gives it a slight advantage and leaves the lion scrambling to turn or keep up.

This battle between the zebra and lion might last less than a minute.

Zebras and lions can both run more than 30 miles per hour (50 kph).

Zebra Talk
Zebras bark, bray, and snort to communicate.

Fast Felines
Female lions are quicker and more agile than males.

Foot Size
A zebra's hoof is about the size of a grapefruit.

Don't Touch
Porcupines do not shoot their quills. The quills detach easily when a predator touches them.

Fisher Food
Despite their name, fishers rarely eat fish. They eat small animals like rabbits, snowshoe hares, squirrels, and raccoons.

Heads Up
Porcupines climb up trees to escape. A fisher can run down a tree headfirst to attack its prey from above.

KEEP AWAY

A predator has 30,000 reasons to avoid a North American porcupine. That's how many needle-sharp quills cover a porcupine's back, sides, and tail. When touched, the quills sink into the predator's skin. This painful defense keeps most predators away.

Except a fisher. It uses a different strategy. This member of the weasel family dashes in and bites the porcupine's face. It quickly dodges the porcupine's quills. The fisher bites the porcupine over and over, weakening its prey. Then, the fisher flips the porcupine on its back. This exposes the porcupine's unprotected underside.

Toe pads help the frog hold on to the tree.

Size Wise
There are almost 400 species of flying frogs. The largest ones are a little longer than the palm of a child's hand. The smallest ones are about the length of a kid's pinky finger.

Some prey don't have body armor, but they do have an instant escape plan.

The Wallace's flying frog lives high up in rainforest trees. This shiny, green amphibian hunts insects. When a hungry, tree-climbing snake slithers in its direction, the frog leaps out of the tree. Instead of plummeting to the ground, this escape artist glides away. The frog holds out its legs and spreads its webbed toes. It catches air and coasts like a tiny parachute. The frog can steer as it glides. It drifts about 50 feet (15 m), the length of a semi-truck, and lands in another tree.

Warning Signs
Porcupines chatter their teeth when threatened.

13

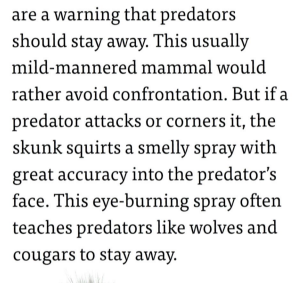

Owls swoop in and eat skunks. The big, silent birds fly down and grab the skunk before they can react.

Slam Dunk Spray
A skunk can spray at something that's 15 feet (4.6 m) away. That's the distance from the free-throw line to the basketball hoop.

A skunk's black and white stripes are a warning that predators should stay away. This usually mild-mannered mammal would rather avoid confrontation. But if a predator attacks or corners it, the skunk squirts a smelly spray with great accuracy into the predator's face. This eye-burning spray often teaches predators like wolves and cougars to stay away.

Born Ready
Baby skunks can spray when they are just about three weeks old.

14

A tamandua eats as many as 9,000 termites and ants a day.

The tamandua, a kind of anteater that lives in South America, sends away predators with a stinky spray, too. With a spray said to be four times stronger than a skunk's, the tamandua can keep predators like jaguars, cougars, margays, owls, and eagles at a distance.

And with claws as long as a grizzly bear's, the tamandua has even more defenses. On the ground, it rears up onto its back legs. It uses its tail for balance, like a kickstand. It lashes out with its strong arms and claws. If attacked in a tree, the tamandua hangs by its tail so its arms can take a swing at the predator.

Skunk Predator
Owls do not have a good sense of smell, which might help them prey on skunks.

Slurp!
If your tongue were as long as a tamandua's, you could easily lick the back of your neck.

15

Snake Speed
Black mambas can slither faster than the average human runs.

Protective Scales
Thick scales protect the snake eagle's legs and feet from the mamba's bite, but the bird needs to be careful and quick.

The black mamba is one of the fastest and deadliest snakes in the world. It would prefer to avoid conflict but strikes when threatened. It rises up, spreads its hood wide, and opens its mouth, showing off the black color inside. If that defensive stance doesn't work, the snake bites its attacker over and over again, injecting it with deadly venom. The toxic venom can kill a human-size animal within 20 minutes.

Snake eagles also hunt puff adders and boomslangs, both extremely venomous snakes.

A black mamba can be as long as a car.

But the black mamba's size, speed, and deadly bite don't stop predators from trying to eat it. Snake eagles perch in trees and watch for snakes. In a fast and nimble attack, the snake eagle flies in and grabs the mamba with its sharp talons. While it is still flying, the bird immediately tears off the most dangerous part of the snake: its head. Then, it swallows the snake whole. But if the bird's timing is off or it isn't quick enough, the mamba's venom will kill it.

Bad Bite
A black mamba has up to 20 drops of venom in each fang. It only takes two drops to kill a human-size animal.

Wide Wings
A snake eagle's wingspan is wider than a child's arm span.

On the Hunt
Black mambas hunt mice, rats, birds, and squirrels.

OUT OF SIGHT

Camouflage helps lessen the chance that a predator will see its prey. Staying hidden is one of the most common kinds of defenses. Animals have different kinds of camouflage.

Some blend into the background. A peppered moth's wings match the bark and lichens that grow on the trees where they land. When the moth stops moving, it's nearly impossible for its predators, like robins and nuthatches, to see it.

Foot Feathers Feathers on the ptarmigan's feet keep it warm and work like snowshoes to help keep the bird from sinking in the snow.

A ptarmigan's camouflage works so well that it's hard to see even from just a few feet away.

Rock ptarmigans (TAR-ma-gens) live in the Arctic. These birds make their nest and find their food on the ground. They molt, or lose their feathers, to match the changes that the seasons bring to their surroundings. Their plumage is white in the winter and brown in the summer. This camouflage makes it harder for predators like polar bears, arctic foxes, snowy owls, and wolverines to see them.

Pass the Pepper
The peppered moth's name describes the dark spots on its wings.

Midnight Meal
Most moths hunt at night and hide during the day to avoid hungry predators.

Sambar deer are a favorite prey of tigers. These big cats can imitate the deer's "pook" sound to lure them closer.

Arm's Length
A leafy sea dragon is about 18 inches (46 cm) long. That's about the length from an adult's fingertips to her elbow.

Predators hide, too, to stay out of their prey's sight.

Tigers have orange and black stripes that blend into the lights, shadows, and vegetation where they live. When these big cats see their prey, they silently stalk on padded paws until they are close enough to launch an attack. Wary prey like deer and wild boar will quickly run if they sense that this powerful predator is nearby.

Like tigers, leafy sea dragons use camouflage to stay concealed. These seahorse relatives can't swim very well. But their leaf-like fins and frilly limbs mimic the seaweed that their prey, small shrimp, call home. They even sway and move like floating seaweed. Leafy sea dragons can also change color to blend in even better.

Seafood Feast
Leafy sea dragons suck in prey through their long snout. They eat thousands of small shrimp a day.

Overlooked
Leafy sea dragons have few predators because they're hard to see.

DECEPTIVE DISGUISES

Camouflage helps protect prey from predators.

The bird-dropping spider looks like something a predator wouldn't eat: bird poo.

Stick insects mimic sticks and twigs. They even move with the wind.

A mossy frog's skin texture and color help it disappear into the surrounding plants.

The small eastern screech owl nests in holes in trees. Its feathers blend in with the bark.

A stonefish looks like a harmless rock as a way to stay hidden from both its prey and predators.

23

Hairy Cousins
Trapdoor spiders are related to tarantulas.

More Trapdoors
There are many kinds of trapdoor spiders. Not all trapdoor spiders make a door for their underground burrows.

IT'S A TRAP!

Trapdoor spiders live alone. They do not build webs to catch food. But they do set a trap.

A trapdoor spider digs a tunnel with its modified fangs. Then, it makes a hinged "door" using dirt, twigs and leaves, and its own silk.

At night, it hunts by opening the door a little. Trip wires made of the spider's silk threads vibrate when prey walk near the door. The spider charges out from its hiding place. It captures prey like crickets, grasshoppers, and beetles with its front legs, and then bites the prey with its venomous fangs.

Trapdoor spiders are about one inch (2.5 cm) long. That's about the size of a child's thumbprint.

Spider Snacks
Trapdoor spiders eat insects and other spiders.

Worldwide
Trapdoor spiders live all over the world.

Spider Nursery
Some wasps drag the immobilized spider to a hole they've dug. Others use the spider's burrow, and some make small nests out of mud.

Baby Food
The trapdoor spider is often bigger than a spider wasp. That provides enough food for the baby spider to eat as it grows.

The trapdoor spider is a predator, but it can also be prey. A shut door keeps most predators from invading the trapdoor spider's home. But it doesn't keep out the spider wasp.

The female wasp hunts the trapdoor spider. The spider holds the trapdoor shut with its fangs. But the female wasp just eats the door!

Once inside, the wasp stuns the spider with her venomous stinger.

She lays an egg on the now-still spider's abdomen. The wasp seals the spider and egg inside the tunnel.

When the baby spider wasp hatches, it eats the still-living spider. About the time it eats its last bit of spider, the baby wraps itself in a cocoon and morphs into an adult wasp.

Long Life
Trapdoor spiders usually live about 20 years. Scientists studied one trapdoor spider that lived for 43 years until a spider wasp killed it.

Delicious Drink
Adult spider wasps drink flower nectar.

Vicious Venom
The spider wasp's venom is so powerful that the trapdoor spider remains paralyzed while the baby slowly eats it.

Many Feet
Some adult sea stars can have 15,000 tube feet.

Sea Star Speed
Some species of sea star can have 40 arms, but these animals crawl slowly over sand and rocks.

Filter Feeder
Small hair-like structures push water over the clam's gills and trap tiny bits of food.

A clam's shell is its armor. When it closes both halves, it's like slamming a door shut, protecting the animal inside. Strong muscles keep the shell closed and make it nearly impenetrable—until a sea star shows up. Sea stars have many feet. Called tube feet, they look like tiny macaroni noodles and work like suction cups to help them pull open clam shells.

sea urchin

The sea star wraps its body around its prey. It uses its tube feet to slowly pull open the clam's shell. It doesn't have to open it very far. A sea star eats by sliding its stomach out of its mouth. It inserts its stomach into the shell to digest the clam hiding inside.

Seafloor Seafood
Sea stars eat mussels, sea urchins, and sand dollars.

Shut Tight
When a clam senses movement, it slams its shell shut. That movement could be a predator.

Big Bird
A cassowary is as tall as a human adult.

High Jump
A cassowary jumps seven feet (2 m) into the air to deliver a kick. That's as tall as a door.

NO CONTEST

Some prey are just too well-armed for most predators.

Cassowaries are large, shy birds that live in Australia's rainforest. They cannot fly. These solitary birds walk through the trees looking for fruit on the forest floor. Each of their feet has one claw that's as long as your index finger. A cassowary uses this claw to dig for fallen fruit. Claws also come in handy for protection.

A cassowary usually disappears into the forest rather than fight. But this wary bird turns lethal when cornered. It charges. Then, it delivers a fatal kick with its powerful legs and sharp claws that can slice a predator open.

Like cassowaries, Cape buffalo mind their own business as they munch on grass and travel in enormous herds on the African savanna. They mow down tall grass, which helps other plant eaters get to the shorter grasses they prefer to eat.

Lions, hyenas, leopards, and crocodiles hunt Cape buffalo. But that's a risky, even deadly, pursuit.

Cape buffalo work together to protect younger herd members. They crowd together, creating a wall of armor with their sharp, helmet-like horns. These huge animals gore and trample predators, often killing them.

Best Buffalo Friends
Cape buffalo often sleep with their heads on each other.

Huge Herds
Herds of up to 2,000 buffalo roam the African savanna.

Big Buffalo
A male Cape buffalo weighs as much as, or more than, four lions.

Play Group
Hippo mothers gather with other mothers and calves to provide more protection from predators.

Hippo Predators
Nile crocodiles, hyenas, and lions prey on young hippos.

Like cassowaries and Cape buffalo, hippopotamuses are considered one of the world's most dangerous animals. It's not their hunting skills that make them deadly. Also like cassowaries and Cape buffalo, hippos eat plants. They live in rivers and come onto land at night to eat grass.

These big mammals spend most of the day—up to 16 hours—in the water. Hippos do not swim. They walk or bounce across the river bottom. They can hold their breath for up to five minutes.

Sometimes, they keep their nostrils, eyes, and ears just above the water's surface.

Hippos rule the river. Their size alone makes them formidable. And with a giant mouth full of 20-inch (51-cm)-long teeth, the hippo is almost an unstoppable predator. Hippos are most dangerous in the water, where they aggressively protect themselves, their territory, and their young. A full-grown adult hippo faces few predators.

Hippo Size
Average-size hippos weigh as much as a car. Large males can weigh as much as two cars. Newborn hippos weigh as much as two car tires!

Hippos' Home
Hippos only live in sub-Saharan Africa.

Fierce Hunters
Leopard seals hunt other Antarctic penguins, including macaroni, chinstrap, gentoo, king, and emperor. They also hunt the fur seal, crabeater seal, and Weddell seal pups.

Sizable Seals
Leopard seals can weigh 1,000 pounds (454 kg). That's as much as a big motorcycle.

POLAR PREDATORS

Apex predators shape habitats. That's because the fear of this top predator's presence changes how prey behave, including where and when they eat. Apex predators have few, if any, predators themselves.

Leopard seals share more than just a spotted coat with the big cat they are named for. These fierce mammals are expert hunters. Unlike other seals that prey on cold-blooded animals like fish, leopard seals feed on warm-blooded prey, including other seals. Among their favorite prey are Adélie penguins.

These penguins come onshore to lay their eggs and raise their chicks. The birds return to the ocean to hunt.

Penguins have wings, but they use them to swim and dive. These birds cannot fly.

Adélies swim fast and dive deep, but they don't have many defenses against leopard seals. These large predators swim under or along the edges of floating ice in the frigid waters of Antarctica looking for Adélies. The seals snatch the penguins as they hop in or out of the water. Leopard seals also burst through thin ice to grab penguins walking above them. Or they catch them in the water, sinking their sharp teeth into their prey.

Sightseeing
Leopard seals live in Antarctic waters. But some travel long distances. One was observed in the southern part of the Great Barrier Reef, Australia.

Killer Whales
Orcas are leopard seals' only known predator.

Fishy Food
Adélie penguins hunt fish and krill.

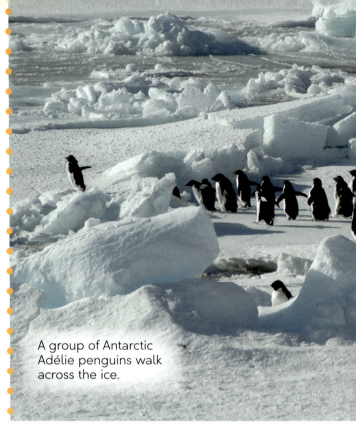

A group of Antarctic Adélie penguins walk across the ice.

Small Bird
An Adélie penguin is as long as a child's leg.

Adélies change their behavior to avoid leopard seals. They hunt during the day, but not because they can't see in the dark. They often hunt deep in the sea where it is dark all the time. The birds don't hunt at night because that's when leopard seals are awake. The seals sleep during the middle of the day. Fewer seals in the water means less chance of an encounter with the penguin-eating predator.

A Cold Swim
Adélie penguins swim thousands of miles a year, but they stay in Antarctic and sub-Antarctic waters.

Look at Me!
Adult Adélie penguins have white rings around their eyes.

When some penguins on Ross Island in Antarctica return from hunting, they take the long way back to their chicks. Instead of swimming, the birds get out of the water on the other side of the island. Then, they waddle three miles (5 km) back home. They do this to avoid the leopard seals that are waiting closer to the colony.

37

Bats Abound
There are about 1,400 kinds of bats. They are found on every continent except Antarctica.

Flying Mammal
Bats are mammals, like you, and the only mammal that can fly.

Buzzing Bats
Bats are prey, too. Owls hunt greater mouse-eared bats. The bats make a buzzing sound that might mimic hornets to keep owls away.

DINNER IN THE DARK

Bats silently and swiftly soar through the air. They twist and turn in the dark as easily as a bird flies in the daytime. Bats rely on echolocation to find food and their way in the dark.

Echolocation is using sound to see. The bat sends out beams of high-pitched sound. When the sound hits something, like an insect, the sound bounces back to the bat. Using echolocation, the bat can sense how far away the insect is, its size, and which way it's moving. Then, the bat swoops in and gobbles up its prey.

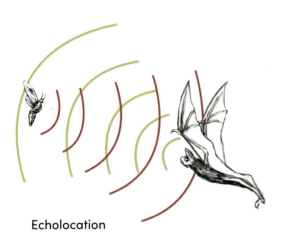

Echolocation

A mother bat with a baby to feed catches 4,000 insects a night.

Listening to Leaves
Common big-eared bats hover as they echolocate. They can tell the difference between an empty leaf and one with an insect on it.

Bug Eater
Insect-eating bats hunt flies, beetles, butterflies, moths, and other insects. Some, like big-eared bats, eat lizards.

39

Hearing Help
Bats have big ears and flaps and wrinkles around their nose and face. These features help them hear the echoes.

Moths have found many ways to combat bats' echolocation skills. Some drop to the ground and hide when they hear a bat. Some moths will zigzag, loop, and dive when they hear a bat.

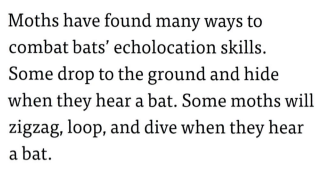

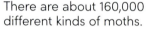
There are about 160,000 different kinds of moths.

Long-Distance Listening
Some moths can hear an echolocating bat a football field away.

Scales on a moth's wings help it fly.

Sound Barrier The scales on some moths can absorb up to 70 percent of a bat's echolocation sound.

Some moths can hide from the bat's sound beam. Scales cover a moth's wings. Some moths' scales can help absorb the sound, rather than letting it bounce back to the bat.

Scales can also muffle the sound, lowering the strength of the returning echo. The scales kind of turn down the volume on the bat's echo, making it harder for the bat to find the moth.

Breaking Free The scales can also help a moth escape a spiderweb.

41

Munch on Lunch
Elk eat grass, tree bark, twigs, and any plant parts they can find in the winter.

Heavyweight
One large male elk weighs as much as six large gray wolves.

Keeping Pace
Elk and wolves can both run about 40 miles per hour (64 kph) for short distances.

FINDING BALANCE

Depending on where they live, wolves often hunt large, hooved animals such as elk, deer, and moose. But these prey have many ways to avoid wolves. They have excellent vision, hearing, and sense of smell. They can run fast over long distances.

Super Smellers
When wolves stand downwind to catch the scent of prey, they can smell something three football fields away.

Hunting is a deadly challenge for a wolf. Hunting takes a lot of energy. The elk, moose, and other large prey they hunt are quick and agile. Plus, these animals can deliver a painful, even deadly, kick with their sharp hooves.

Like many predators, wolves do not eat every day. They gorge themselves after a hunt, with each wolf eating as much as 20 pounds (9 kg) of meat. That's like you eating 80 quarter-pound hamburgers for dinner once a week! Then, the wolves do not hunt for several days.

Hungry Pups
Mothers and pups need to eat about three times more food than other wolves.

Wild Wolves
Today, about 500 wolves live in and around Yellowstone Park. They are an important part of the ecosystem.

Competition
Elk compete for food and space with bison, moose, bighorn sheep, deer, and pronghorn.

Lots of Elk
As many as 40,000 elk live in and around Yellowstone. More elk live there than any other mammal.

The relationship between wolves and their prey is an excellent example of how predators and prey are essential to creating balance in an ecosystem. The removal of one can cause dramatic changes.

Overhunting, competition for food and space, and a lack of understanding of the wolves' role in the ecosystem caused these animals to be hunted to extinction in many places.

For nearly 100 years, there were no wolves in Yellowstone National Park, USA. Without the wolves, the elk population grew. Then, the population drastically dropped when the elk starved due to lack of food or severe weather.

Wolves hunt and live in groups called packs. Packs average about 12 animals.

About 30 years ago, wolves were reintroduced to Yellowstone. Some people feared that the wolves would eat all the elk and other prey animals.

That didn't happen. Instead, the wolves hunted the old, weaker, and ill animals. This made the elk population stronger and healthier. It also helped the elk population remain a steady size rather than growing and then drastically dropping.

Life isn't easy for predators or prey. But both of their roles in an ecosystem are essential. The balance between the hunter and the hunted is often complex and delicate, but it is essential to the survival of predators, prey, and their homes.

Leftovers
The wolves' hunting skills benefit other animals. Bears successfully chase wolves away from their catch. Coyotes and other animals eat the leftovers after the wolves leave.

Home to Many
Many animals live in Yellowstone, including nearly 300 bird species, 67 mammal species, plus fish, reptiles, and amphibians.

GLOSSARY

Amphibian
A group of cold-blooded animals with backbones

Camouflage
Using coloring or covering to match the surroundings

Cold-blooded
An animal that cannot produce its own heat; its body temperature changes with the temperature around it

Echolocation
A method by which some animals, like bats, find objects using reflected, or echoed, sound

Ecosystem
Interactions between plants, animals, and the environment where they live

Habitat
A place where animals live

Overhunting
Removing animals faster than they can reproduce and maintain a healthy population

Predator
Animals that hunt and eat other animals

Prey
Animals that are hunted by predators

Seaweed
A kind of algae; it gets its energy from sunlight but does not have roots

Venom
A toxin that an animal injects through a bite or a sting

Warm-blooded
An animal that can produce its own heat, regardless of the temperature around it

INDEX

Adélie penguins 34–37
anteaters 15
apex predators 34
arctic foxes 6, 18
bats 38–41
bears 6, 45
bird-dropping spiders 22
black mambas 16–17
brown bears 6
camouflage 18–23
Cape buffalo 30, 31, 32
cassowaries 30, 32
clams 28–29
common big-eared bats 39
coyotes 45
crocodiles 31, 32
deer 20, 42, 44
eagles 6, 15, 16, 17
echolocation 38, 39, 40
ecosystem 6, 44, 45
elk 42, 43, 44–45

fishers 12
frogs 13, 23
greater mouse-eared bats 38
herd protection 8, 9, 31
hippopotamuses 32–33
honey badgers 6
hyenas 8, 31, 32
killer whales 35
ladybugs 6, 7
leafy sea dragons 20, 21
leopard seals 34–37
lions 8–11, 31, 32
mossy frogs 23
moths 18, 19, 39, 40–41
orcas 35
owls 14, 15, 19, 38
penguins 34–37
peppered moth 18, 19
porcupines 12, 13
predator versus prey 6–11
ptarmigans 18, 19

rock ptarmigans 18, 19
sambar deer 20
sea stars 28–29
seals 34–37
skunks 14
snake eagles 16, 17
snakes 13, 16–17
spider wasps 26–27
spiders 22, 24–27, 41
stick insects 22
stonefish 23
tamanduas 15
tarantulas 24
tigers 20
trapdoor spiders 24–27
Wallace's flying frogs 13
wasps 26–27
whale sharks 6, 7
wolves 14, 42–45
Yellowstone National Park, USA 44–45
zebras 8–11

QUIZ

Answer the questions to see what you have learned. Check your answers in the key below.

1. True or False: Porcupines shoot their quills.
2. How does a sea star open a clam?
3. Which animal looks like seaweed?
4. Where do hippos live?
5. Why do some moths drop when they hear a bat?
6. Why do Adélie penguins hunt during the day?
7. What is the main food for wolves in Yellowstone?
8. What do cassowaries eat?

1. False 2. It pulls it open with its tube feet 3. A leafy sea dragon
4. In rivers 5. To avoid being detected by the bat's echolocation
6. Leopard seals sleep during the day 7. Elk 8. Fruit